the book of
ice cream

lydia capasso
simone de feo

the book of
ice cream

lydia capasso
simone de feo

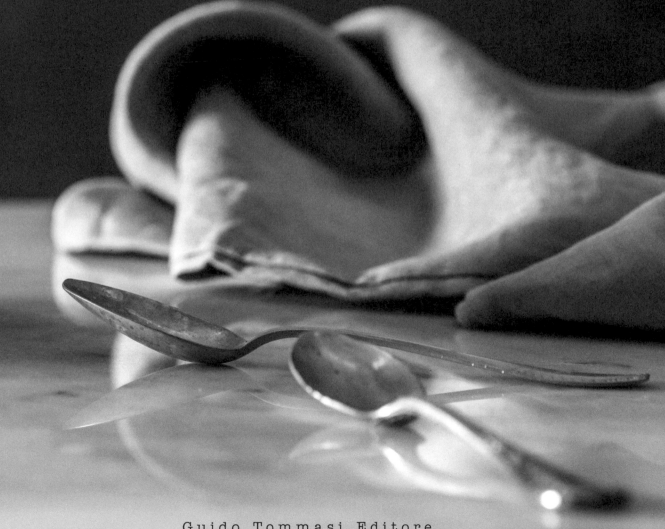

Guido Tommasi Editore

Contents

WHY THIS BOOK

I could live on ice cream, I could eat it until I burst. Put me in front of a tub of hazelnut flavour and I'll finish it only when I have scraped the bottom, right down to the very last spoonful. When I was a child, I was the proud owner of a toy ice cream parlor: in order to cream the mixture I only had to lift and lower a plastic plunger in the shape of a candied cherry. Those trial blobs of iced cream were my first culinary successes (or failures). If I think about it, that's where it all began. My love for cooking, good food and everything else connected comes from a toy. Being a real "foodie", I am always looking for the perfect ice cream, even in the ice cream parlor. The perfect hazelnut flavour, a fruit ice cream that really tastes of fruit, or a true custard flavour.

One day, during the course of my investigations, I bumped into Simone De Feo, a passionate expert ice cream maker, who makes ice cream just how I like it: creamy, enveloping and delicious, exactly how for years I've tried to make it at home with a normal home ice cream maker. The idea of this book is to combine his skills and professionalism with my passion for food and experimenting, to show how anyone can make good ice cream, the best that can be made with amateur equipment, at home.

To eat a tasty ice cream or a refreshing granita (snow cone), it really isn't necessary to go out and buy one: ice cream is a dessert that is quick and easy to make, it can even be a rapid solution for the end of a meal. Imagine having guests for dinner and while you are at the table enjoying your friends, the ice cream maker does its job and prepares dessert. Use the best ingredients, seasonal fruit, fresh milk, eggs from happy hens that you serve every day. If you don't have an ice cream maker, don't worry! We'll explain some tricks to get around this problem.

Lydia Capasso

In the preface to this book dedicated to ice cream, you're probably expecting to read all about how my passion began, how it has guided me in the creation and selection of recipes that, seven years ago, led me to give up my career as a computer technician to launch myself in the adventure of the Cremeria Capolinea ice cream parlor in Reggio Emilia with my partner Monica. My ardent wish is for this book to convey a real sense of family, the embrace of memories, because my story begins at home, in my mother's kitchen, from a most unexpected flavour.

A highlight of my childhood was the discovery of confectioner's custard. It was my first time at the hob, and I was about 6 or 7 years old. I remember that from time to time my mother prepared a kind of confectioner's custard as a snack. I thought it was delicious, so I decided to ask her to teach me how to make it. Making this custard was enormously satisfying for me (I could decide how much to make…and I always made vast quantities!), but it there was a drawback that prevented me from eating it straightaway: it was too hot! Urged on by childish impatience, I would put it in the freezer and wait.

This waiting time seemed like eternity. It was on one of these afternoons spent in the kitchen between the hob and the TV that it all began. One day, I prepared two bowls of custard but I left one in the freezer for too long and so it was partially frozen. When I went to get it out to wolf it down, I saw there was a problem, but I was not to be beaten: I mixed it until it became smooth. I realised that it had

transformed itself into a mixture that was not liquid, but neither frozen: it was something like ice cream. At that moment, my passion for custard ice cream came about and even today, it remains my favorite.

My curiosity and passion continued; they still continue to accompany me today in my personal quest for "good ice cream": ice cream in which flavour prevails. More important than structure and the preservability, it is taste that guides me, whether I am creating more traditional flavours or searching for a balance between unexpected aromatic notes, bringing savoury into the ice cream, creating recipes that amaze, redefine the concept of traditional ice cream and open the doors to new unheard-of possibilities.

Easy to digest, not too sweet, balanced in the mouth and that leaves the palate clean after eating. Even the taste of the most creative ice cream cannot ignore the most genuine Italian tradition to which I am inextricably linked and which, thanks to the help of Lydia Capasso, expert and great ice cream enthusiast, you can now reproduce autonomously in your own kitchen. I consider the selection of principal ingredients one of the most important phases of preparation: only by using the best, seasonal and local, can ice cream become a narrator for the area and tell entire stories on the palate.

Being true to tradition is the solid base on which to blend creativity and taste with innovation. This is the path I have chosen to follow in order to create ice creams with extremely short recipes but of great aromatic richness. Without semi-finished products, synthetic flavourings, emulsifiers, refined or hydrogenated vegetable fats, I am sharing my recipes with you to offer you ice cream of the highest artisanal tradition.
Happy creating and happy tasting!

Simone De Feo

A LITTLE BIT OF HISTORY

The world is full of ice cream parlors that pass themselves off as guardians, as well as sellers of real Italian ice cream. The truth is that outside of Italy, ice cream is adored and diffused almost as much as pizza and pasta, and, like pizza and pasta, is associated with traditional Italian cuisine. Whether right or wrong, ice cream is thought of as one of our gastronomic glories, and we do nothing to dispel this.

Here is not the place in which to argue at length about its origins, or rather, this was not our aim, but we are happy to take the opportunity to make a short digression. We can only begin with its primordial form: the sorbet; an iced mixture of ice and sugar which has been around since the dawn of time. The first Arab conquerors brought it to Sicily between the 9th and 11th centuries. Its name derives from the Arabic *sherbet* (fresh drink) or *sharber* (to sip). In Sicily it was made by mixing snow from Mount Etna that was collected and guarded by "*nivaroli*" (it is not by chance that the best granitas are still found on the eastern side of the island). Then, in Renaissance times, sorbets became all the rage in the courts. When, in 1533, Catherine de Medici left Florence to become the wife of the man who would one day unexpectedly become King of France with the name of Henry III, the consecration of this iced dessert became permanent.

It is said that Catherine brought cooks, pastry chefs and an ice cream maker to the Parisian court.
It seems that we should be thanking Tuscany for the first iced creams, in particular Bernardo Buontalenti, engineer, architect, sculptor, theatre set designer, who was active in the court of great Dukes of Tuscany in the second half of the sixteenth century. He was the inventor behind a "technological" machine with blades, worked by a handle, which creamed together a mixture of milk, honey and eggs. Once again, the French were amazed by this latest iced invention, which was used at the wedding banquet of another Medici, Maria. She was married to Henry IV of Borbone by proxy at the Palazzo Vecchio in October 1600.

But the true father of Italian ice cream is thought to be Procopio dei Coltelli, a Sicilian cook and pastry chef who moved to Paris. There, in 1686, he opened Caffè Procope, which soon became famous for its "iced waters" and ice creams.

Before entering into this question, it's a good idea
to clarify straightaway the differences between
the "creams" or the iced combinations that exist.

ice cream

An ice cream is an iced mixture that is creamed, with the presence of animal fats and proteins.

semi-freddo

A semi-freddo has a higher percentage of fats and sugar compared to ice cream. It is not creamed and is usually shaped.

sorbet

The sorbet, or nowadays what we intend to be a sorbet, is very similar to a granita, or snow cone, but it has more sugar, is more airy (it is creamed) and is generally served at lower temperatures (-10/-12°/14°F, 10.4°F).

granita
or snow cone

A granita is an iced mixture of water and sugar with a characterizing element. It does not generally incorporate air, even if with the help of an ice cream maker it is made more quickly.

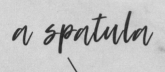

a spatula

an ice cream maker
with compressor and
storage container

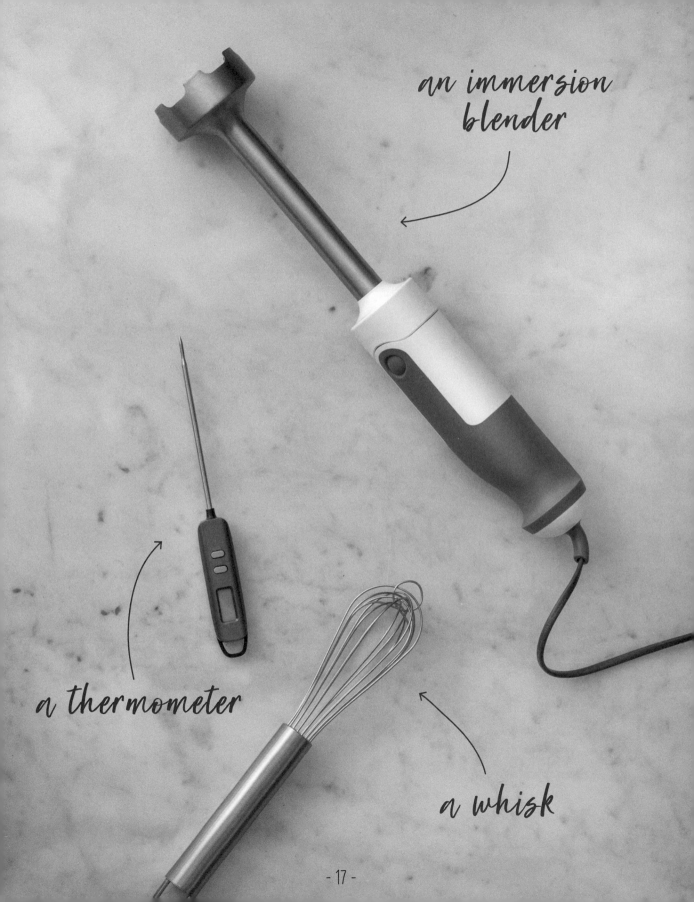

an immersion blender

a thermometer

a whisk

SUGARS

Sugars provide structure, creaminess and lower the freezing point of a mixture.
Not all sugars behave in the same way: caster, raw and whole (saccharose) can be interchangeable. Honey and agave sugar have equal weight, are sweeter and also have a superior anti-freezing power. Trehalose has the same anti-freezing power as saccharose.

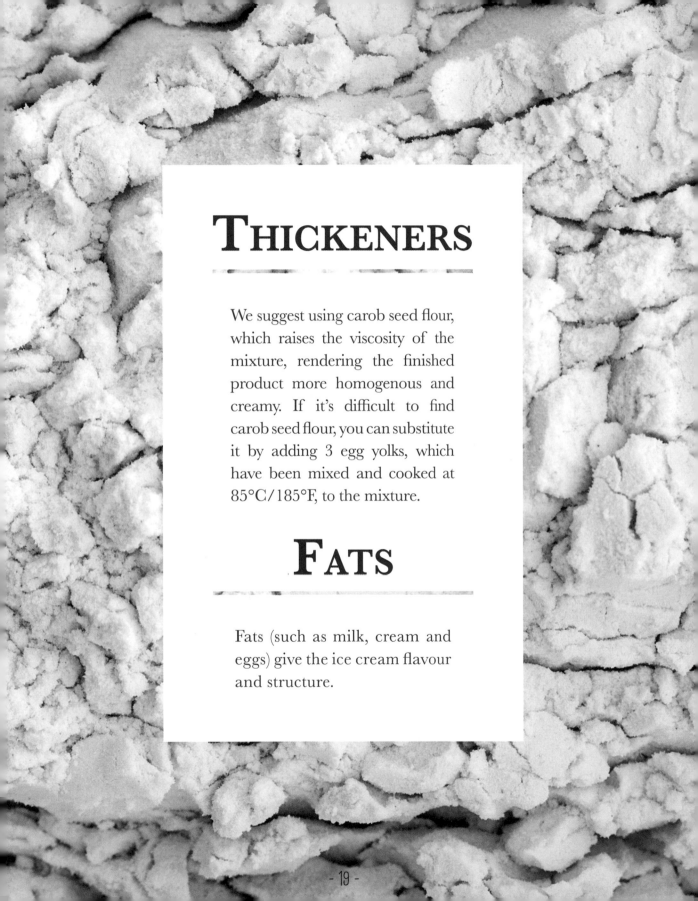

THICKENERS

We suggest using carob seed flour, which raises the viscosity of the mixture, rendering the finished product more homogenous and creamy. If it's difficult to find carob seed flour, you can substitute it by adding 3 egg yolks, which have been mixed and cooked at 85°C/185°F, to the mixture.

FATS

Fats (such as milk, cream and eggs) give the ice cream flavour and structure.

IF YOU DON'T HAVE AN ICE CREAM MAKER

This doesn't apply to granitas: you only need a fork. The mixture indicated in the recipe is poured into a container with low sides, metal if possible, which is put into the freezer to rest for 1 to 2 hours. With the help of a fork, break the layer of ice that will have formed on the surface, and mix. Put it back in the freezer and repeat the operation every half hour, at least 5 or 6 times, until a soft, homogenous but granular mixture is obtained. Finally, when the liquid has almost completely frozen, grate harder, and the granita will be ready.

For ice cream, however, get hold of some ice trays. The stated mixture in the recipe will be frozen in special moulds. Before serving, just get the cubes of frozen cream out of the freezer and blend them. You'll see crumbs at first, but just mix with a spoon until you get a creamy frozen mixture.

How to serve it

You will have noted that if you bring home a tub of ice cream bought in an ice cream parlor, and you put it in the freezer, it has a tendency to harden.
This happens because home freezers reach lower temperatures compared to professional ones.
In the same way, when you prepare ice cream at home, you'll realise that it has the right consistency if you eat it as soon as it is made, but if you keep it in the freezer, it becomes very compact. Remember to keep it in the fridge for 2 to 3 hours before eating it.

milk

———————   ———————

Milk ice cream

Chocolate chunk ice cream

Panna cotta ice cream

Mascarpone and fig ice cream

Ricotta, honey and rosemary ice cream

Mascarpone, lemon and pine nut ice cream

Mascarpone, capers and coffee ice cream

Yogurt, ginger and blueberry stripe ice cream

Yogurt, extra-virgin olive oil and thyme ice cream

Yogurt and honey ice cream

Robiola, honey and pear ice cream

———————   ———————

Milk
ice cream

690 G/23 FL OZ/2.5 CUPS FRESH WHOLE MILK
100 G/3.5 FL OZ/½ CUP FRESH CREAM
200 G/8 OZ/1 CUP CASTER SUGAR
2 G/0.1 OZ CAROB SEED FLOUR

———————— ————————

Mix the cream with the milk in a
saucepan and place it over the heat. Add
the sugar and carob seed flour. Check
the temperature with a thermometer
and wait for the mixture to reach
85°C/185°F. Cool quickly and put it in
the ice cream maker.

MILK

Milk ice cream has many variations and interpretations.

It is a neutral base that can be enriched with lemon zest and basil leaves, cinnamon, vanilla and orange or with star anise and mint, blended and mixed with the milk.

Chocolate chunk ice cream

INGREDIENTS

690 G/23 FL OZ/2.5 CUPS FRESH WHOLE MILK

100 G/3.5 FL OZ/½ CUP FRESH CREAM

200 G/8 OZ/1 CUP CASTER SUGAR

2 G/0.1 OZ CAROB SEED FLOUR

100 G/4 OZ DARK CHOCOLATE

————————— —————————

Milk is also the base for chocolate chunk icc cream. Follow the procedure for the preparation of milk ice cream (p. 28); after the creaming stage, simply add the chopped dark chocolate. Alternatively, you can melt the chocolate and let it drip over the ice cream after creaming.

Panna cotta ice cream

300 G/10 FL OZ SWEETENED CONDENSED MILK
670 G/22 FL OZ/2.8 CUPS FRESH WHOLE MILK
20 G/JUST UNDER 1 OZ CASTER SUGAR
2 G/0.1 OZ CAROB SEED FLOUR

Bring together the condensed milk and the fresh milk, mix carefully, add the sugar and the carob seed flour. Place over a medium heat and bring to 85°C/185°F. Allow to cool quickly and pour into an ice cream maker. Switch on and leave to work until the ice cream reaches the correct consistency.

Mascarpone and fig ice cream

INGREDIENTS

150 g/6 oz MASCARPONE CHEESE

125 g/5 oz DRIED FIGS

110 g/JUST OVER 4 oz CASTER SUGAR

600 g/20.5 FL oz/2.5 CUPS FRESH WHOLE MILK

2 g/0.1 oz CAROB SEED FLOUR

Roughly chop the dried figs, place in a saucepan with the mascarpone, milk, sugar and carob seed flour then heat. Remove from the heat and blend with the help of an immersion blender. Heat again and bring to 85°C/185°F. Quickly cool the mixture and place in the ice cream maker.

MILK

Ricotta, honey and rosemary ice cream

INGREDIENTS

760 G/25.8 FL OZ/3.2 CUPS FRESH WHOLE MILK

70 G/2.5 OZ SUGAR

100 G/4 OZ RICOTTA CHEESE

70 G/2.5 OZ WILDFLOWER, ACACIA
  OR ORANGE HONEY

1 G/0.05 OZ ROSEMARY

2 G/0.1 OZ CAROB SEED FLOUR

_____ _____

Blend the needles of the rosemary in a saucepan with the milk and sugar. Place over a medium heat. Add the ricotta, honey and carob seed flour. Stir continuously until the temperature reaches 85°C/185°F. Then cool quickly and pour the mixture into the ice cream maker.

Mascarpone, lemon and pine nut ice cream

Ingredients

100 g/4 oz mascarpone cheese

200 g/8 oz caster sugar

600 g/20.5 fl oz/2.5 cups fresh whole milk

2 g/0.1 oz carob seed flour

The grated zest of 1 unwaxed lemon

60 g/just over 2 oz pine nuts

Toast the pine nuts, put them in a mixer and blend until a paste is obtained (for the right consistency see p. 200). In a saucepan, mix the mascarpone with the sugar, the milk, the carob seed flour, the lemon zest and the pine nut paste. Place over the heat and stir continuously. Use a thermometer to check the temperature: remove the mixture from the heat when it reaches 85°C/185°F. Cool quickly and place in the ice cream maker.

Mascarpone, capers and coffee ice cream

INGREDIENTS

150 G/6 OZ MASCARPONE CHEESE

200 G/8 OZ CASTER SUGAR

800 G/27 FL OZ/3.4 CUPS FRESH WHOLE MILK

180 G/7 OZ COFFEE GRANULES, ROUGHLY CHOPPED
   OR GROUND FOR A MOKA POT

2 G/0.1 OZ CAROB SEED FLOUR

3 G/0.12 SALTED CAPERS

_____

Remove the salt from the capers in a glass of cold water then drain well. Leave the coffee to infuse in boiling milk for about 5 minutes (no longer or the milk will become bitter) then filter. In a saucepan, blend the milk with the mascarpone, sugar, carob seed flour and the capers. Heat to 85°C/185°F, cool quickly and pour into the ice cream maker.

MILK

Yogurt, ginger and blueberry stripe ice cream

INGREDIENTS

750 g/26.5 oz fresh whole yogurt

20 g/just under 1 oz grated ginger

200 g/8 oz caster sugar

2 g/0.1 oz carob seed flour

100 g/4 oz blueberry compote

———————— ————————

Mix the sugar with the ginger. Place the yogurt, carob seed flour and flavoured sugar in a saucepan, stir carefully to ensure the mixture is homogenous. Keep over the heat until the temperature reaches 85°C/185°F. Remove from the heat and cool quickly before pouring into the ice cream maker. When the mixture is ready, add the blueberry compote and mix well.

Yogurt and ginger ice cream can be made with different variegations: instead of blueberry compote you could use blackberry or fruits of the forest.

Yogurt, extra-virgin olive oil and thyme ice cream

INGREDIENTS

750 G/26.5 OZ FRESH WHOLE YOGURT

200 G/8 OZ CASTER SUGAR

2 G/0.1 OZ CAROB SEED FLOUR

20 G/JUST UNDER 1 OZ EXTRA-VIRGIN OLIVE OIL

3 G/0.12 OZ THYME

——————————— ———————————

With the help of an immersion blender, combine the thyme with the yogurt then place over a medium heat. Gradually add the sugar and carob seed flour, stirring continuously. Leave on the heat until the mixture reaches 85°C/185°F. Then remove from the heat and leave to cool, making sure you add the oil only when the mixture is cold. Mix well and pour into the ice cream maker.

Yogurt and honey ice cream

INGREDIENTS

850 g/29 fl oz/3.6 cups fresh whole yogurt

150 g/6 oz honey

2 g/0.1 oz carob seed flour

Combine the yogurt and the honey in a saucepan, mix well and place over a medium heat. Stir and add the carob seed flour. Stir continuously and bring to 85°C/185°F. Remove from the heat and cool quickly, then pour the mixture into the ice cream maker. Switch on and work until the ideal consistency is reached.

100 G/4 OZ ROBIOLA CHEESE

300 G/12 OZ PEARS

2 G/0.1 OZ CAROB SEED FLOUR

500 G/17 FL OZ/2.1 CUPS FRESH WHOLE MILK

100 G/4 OZ HONEY

_____ _____

Cut the pears into pieces, combine with the robiola and honey then blend. In the meantime, heat the milk. When the other ingredients are thoroughly combined, add the milk and wait until the temperature reaches 85°C/185°F, stirring from time to time. Allow the mixture to cool quickly before pouring into the ice cream maker.

Robiola, honey and pear ice cream

eggs

———————— ————————

Zabaione ice cream

Basil and lemon ice cream

Malaga sauce ice cream

Almond, honey and saffron ice cream

Vanilla semi-freddo with black cherries

———————— ————————

EGGS

Zabaione ice cream

FOR THE ZABAIONE SAUCE	FOR THE ICE CREAM

100 G/4 OZ EGG YOLKS (ABOUT 5)

100 G/4 OZ CASTER SUGAR

100 G/3.4 FL OZ/0.4 CUPS MARSALA

500 G/17 FL OZ/2.1 CUPS FRESH WHOLE MILK

70 G/5 OZ CASTER SUGAR

70 G/2.4 FL OZ/0.3 CUPS CREAM

60 G/JUST OVER 2 OZ EGG YOLKS (ABOUT 3)

Prepare the zabaione sauce: using a whisk, beat the egg yolks with the sugar in a bowl (a metal or glass bowl is better, as you can use this as a bain-marie) until the consistency becomes foamy. Slowly add the Marsala and continue to stir. When the mixture is homogenous, heat some water in a saucepan, place the bowl containing the mixture inside, taking care to check the temperature of the water does not go over 85°C/185°F. Then remove from the heat and cool.

For the ice cream: combine the milk with the cream in a pan and heat; switch off the heat before the mixture boils. In another pan, combine the zabaione sauce, egg yolks and the sugar; beat with a whisk. Slowly add the milk and cream mixture, continue to beat while heating to 85°C/185°F. Remove from the heat, cool quickly and place in the ice cream maker.

Basil and lemon ice cream

INGREDIENTS

600 G/20.5 FL OZ/2.5 CUPS FRESH WHOLE MILK

100 G/3.4 FL OZ/0.4 CUPS CREAM

200 G/8 OZ CASTER SUGAR

100 G/4 OZ EGG YOLKS (ABOUT 5)

2 G/0.1 OZ CAROB SEED FLOUR

10 BASIL LEAVES

THE ZEST OF ½ A LEMON

Mix the sugar, basil leaves and lemon zest in a bowl. Pour the milk, egg yolks and cream into a saucepan then beat with a whisk. Continue to whisk while heating, and bring the mixture to 85°C/185°F. Add the aromatized sugar and the carob seed flour. When the mixture is homogenous, remove from the heat and cool rapidly. Switch on the ice cream maker and work until you obtain the right consistency.

Malaga sauce ice cream

FOR THE MALAGA SAUCE

100 G/4 OZ EGG YOLKS
  (ABOUT 5)
100 G/8 OZ CASTER SUGAR
70 G/2.4 FL OZ/0.3 CUPS
  MALAGA OR DARK RUM

FOR THE ICE CREAM

100 G/4 OZ SULTANAS
500 G/17 FL OZ/2.5 CUPS FRESH
  WHOLE MILK
70 G/5 OZ CASTER SUGAR
70 G/2.4 FL OZ/0.3 CUPS CREAM
90 G/JUST UNDER 4 OZ EGG YOLKS
  (ABOUT 4)

Prepare the sauce: place the egg yolks and sugar into a bowl. Use a whisk to create a foamy mixture, then add the Malaga wine or rum. Pour some water into a saucepan and heat. Place the bowl in the water and warm the egg yolks and sugar mixture in this bain-marie. Use a thermometer to check that the mixture does not exceed 85°C/185°F. Leave to cool and set aside. For the ice cream: soak the sultanas in some water for about ten minutes. Combine the egg yolks and sugar in a saucepan and beat until the mixture becomes foamy. Add the milk, cream and the Malaga sauce; heat to 85°C/185°F. Once the preparation is complete, add the sultanas, cool quickly and pour the mixture into the ice cream maker.

Almond, honey and saffron ice cream

Ingredients

600 g/20.5 fl oz/2.5 cups fresh whole milk

120 g/just under 5 oz egg yolks (about 6)

150 g/2 oz caster sugar

40 g/just under 2 oz honey

100 g/4 oz almonds

4 or 5 saffron threads

Roughly chop the almonds and put aside. Whisk the egg yolks and sugar in a bowl. Gradually add the milk and heat over a medium flame: while stirring, add the honey, almonds and saffron. Use a thermometer to check the temperature: the mixture mustn't boil and should be removed from the heat once it has reached 85°C/185°F. Quickly cool before pouring into the ice cream maker.

EGGS

Vanilla semi-freddo with black cherries

700 G/23 FL OZ/3
CUPS SEMI-
WHIPPED CREAM
100 G/4 OZ BLACK
CHERRIES

1 G/0.04 OZ SALT
160 G/5.4 FL OZ/0.7 CUPS
CREAM
20 G/JUST UNDER 1 OZ
EGG YOLK (ABOUT 1)
25 G/1 OZ CASTER SUGAR
1 VANILLA POD

70 G/2.4 FL OZ/0.3
CUPS WATER
290 G/JUST UNDER 10
OZ CASTER SUGAR
150 G/6 OZ EGG
WHITES (ABOUT 4)

Begin by preparing the pouring custard: combine the egg yolk, sugar, cream and salt. Mix with a whisk. Place everything into a saucepan and cook until the mixture reaches 82°C/180°F. During cooking, add the vanilla pod. Remove from the heat and cool.

Proceed with the preparation of the Italian meringue. Combine the water with the sugar and cook. Use a thermometer to check the temperature: when the water and sugar reach 110°C/230°F, whip the egg whites until stiff with the help of a mixer. When the syrup has reached 120°C/250°F, remove from the heat and pour it in a fine stream over the egg whites while the mixer is still running. Now pour the cool custard over the meringue mixture and mix with a spatula from high to low, taking care not to let the mixture break down. Finally, incorporate the whipped cream and the black cherries. Pour the mixture into a single large mould or individual moulds lined with oven paper, and leave to rest in the freezer overnight. You can add a base of savoiardi (ladyfinger) biscuits, sponge cake or bisquit (p. 87).

caramel

———————— ————————

TOFFEE SAUCE ICE CREAM

NUT BRITTLE ICE CREAM

CRÈME CARAMEL STRIPE ICE CREAM

TOFFEE ICE CREAM

———————— ————————

CARAMEL

INGREDIENTS

300 G/10 FL OZ/1 CUP TOFFEE SAUCE

700 G/24 FL OZ/2.5 CUPS FRESH WHOLE MILK

2 G/0.1 OZ CAROB SEED FLOUR

20 G/JUST UNDER 1 OZ EGG YOLK (ABOUT 1)

_____ _____

Beat the egg yolk with the milk using a whisk, and place over a medium heat. Add the toffee sauce (p. 181) and the carob seed flour. Mix the ingredients together well. Bring the mixture to 85°C/185°F, using a thermometer to check the temperature. Remove the saucepan from the heat and cool quickly, before pouring it into the ice cream maker.

Toffee sauce ice cream

CARAMEL

Nut brittle ice cream

INGREDIENTS

700 G/24 FL OZ/2.5 CUPS FRESH WHOLE MILK

100 G/3.5 FL OZ/½ CUP CREAM

200 G/8 OZ CASTER SUGAR

2 G/0.1 OZ CAROB SEED FLOUR

200 G/8 OZ NUT BRITTLE

———————— ————————

Break up the nut brittle (p. 203) and chop it roughly. Combine the milk, cream, sugar and the carob seed flour in a saucepan and place over a medium heat. Mix until the mixture reaches 85°C/185°F. At this point, the mixture is ready to be transferred to the ice cream maker: before you do this, cool it quickly to obtain the perfect working temperature. Once it is ready, add the pieces of nut brittle and mix well.

Crème caramel stripe ice cream

INGREDIENTS

600 g/20.5 fl oz/2.5 cups fresh whole milk

90 g/3 fl oz/0.4 cups cream

180 g/7 oz caster sugar

100 g/4 oz egg yolks (about 5)

2 g/0.1 oz carob seed flour

100 g/4 oz caramel sauce

———————— ————————

Beat the egg yolks and the sugar together with a whisk. Gradually add the milk and cream; keep stirring. Heat, adding the carob seed flour, until the mixture reaches 85°C/185°F. Cool quickly and place in the ice cream maker. Once it is ready, add the caramel sauce (p. 182), mix well and serve.

CARAMEL

Toffee ice cream

INGREDIENTS

200 G/6.8 FL OZ/0.8 CUPS TOFFEE
SAUCE (P. 181)
80 G/JUST OVER 3 OZ CASTER SUGAR
650 G/22 FL OZ/2.7 CUPS FRESH
WHOLE MILK
50 G/2 OZ COCOA
2 G/0.1 OZ CAROB SEED FLOUR

Place all the ingredients into a saucepan over a medium heat. Stir well to create a homogenous mixture and continue to cook until the temperature reaches 85°C/185°F. Allow to cool quickly: now it is ready to be worked inside the ice cream maker.

coffee

PROFESSOR'S COFFEE ICE CREAM

COFFEE ICE CREAM

COFFEE AND CINNAMON GRANITA

COFFEE AND CARDAMOM SORBET

Professor's coffee ice cream

770 G/26 FL OZ/3.2 CUPS FRESH WHOLE MILK

80 G/JUST OVER 3 OZ COFFEE GRANULES, ROUGHLY
  CHOPPED OR GROUND FOR A MOKA POT

50 G/2 OZ HAZELNUTS

200 G/8 OZ CASTER SUGAR

2 G/0.1 OZ CAROB SEED FLOUR

Toast the hazelnuts in a saucepan, place them in a
mixer and whizz until the mixture becomes a paste
(p. 200). Put the milk in a pan and bring to the boil.
Pour the milk onto the coffee and leave to infuse for five
minutes (no more, or the taste will be too bitter). Filter
the milk and heat it gently, adding the hazelnut paste,
the flour and the sugar. Use a thermometer to check
that the mixture reaches 85°C/185°F. Once the mixture
is homogenous, allow to cool and place in the ice cream
maker.

Coffee ice cream

INGREDIENTS

800 G/27.2 FL OZ/3.4 CUPS FRESH WHOLE MILK

60 G/2.4 FL OZ/0.25 CUPS CREAM

200 G/8 OZ CASTER SUGAR

2 G/0.1 OZ CAROB SEED FLOUR

110 G/JUST OVER 4 OZ COFFEE GRANULES,
   ROUGHLY CHOPPED OR GROUND FOR A MOKA POT

———————————— ————————————

Bring the milk to the boil and pour over the coffee. Leave to infuse for five minutes, adding 2 g/0.1 oz of star anise, 3 g/0.2 oz of cinnamon or 5 g/0.3 oz of cardamom if desired. Filter the milk and place over a low heat. Gradually add the cream, sugar and flour, stirring continuously, making sure the temperature does not exceed 85°C/185°F. Once this temperature has been reached, cool the mixture quickly and place it in the ice cream maker.

Coffee and cinnamon granita

INGREDIENTS

900 G/30.6 FL OZ/3.8 CUPS WATER

120 G/JUST UNDER 5 OZ COFFEE GRANULES,
  ROUGHLY CHOPPED OR MACINATED FOR A MOKA POT

160 G/JUST OVER 6 OZ CASTER SUGAR

10 G/JUST UNDER ½ OZ CINNAMON

_____ _____

Bring the water to the boil in a saucepan
then pour it over the coffee. Leave to infuse
for 5 minutes then filter. Put it back on the
heat and add the sugar and cinnamon.
Once the temperature has reached
85°C/185°F, remove from the heat, cool
quickly and place in the ice cream maker.

Coffee and cardamom sorbet

INGREDIENTS

830 G/28.2 FL OZ/3.5 CUPS WATER

100 G/4 OZ COFFEE GRANULES, ROUGHLY
  CHOPPED OR MACINATED FOR A MOKA POT

250 G/10 OZ CASTER SUGAR

5 G/0.3 OZ CARDAMOM

2 G/0.1 OZ CAROB SEED FLOUR

Prepare the infusion: bring the water to the boil, pour over the coffee and filter after 5 minutes. Place over a medium heat in a saucepan and gradually add the sugar, carob seed flour and the cardamom. When the mixture reaches 85°C/185°F, remove from the heat and cool then place in the ice cream maker.

chocolate
and cocoa

Cocoa granita

Dark chocolate and liquorice sorbet

Dark chocolate and rum ice cream

White chocolate semi-freddo with passion fruit

White chocolate with sugared pistachio nuts and

passion fruit

Cocoa and orange ice cream

Milk chocolate, toffee and salt ice cream

Cocoa granita

INGREDIENTS

70 G/JUST UNDER 3 OZ BITTER COCOA
160 G/JUST OVER 6 OZ CANE SUGAR
770 G/26 FL OZ/3.2 CUPS WATER

——————————— ———————————

Mix all the ingredients, bring to
85°C/185°F over a medium heat and
cook until the mixture is homogenous.
Then cool quickly and pour into the
ice cream maker to complete the
preparation.

Dark chocolate and liquorice sorbet

150 G/6 OZ DARK 75 % ARRIBA CHOCOLATE

200 G/8 OZ CANE SUGAR

2 G/0.1 OZ CAROB SEED FLOUR

2 G/0.1 OZ SALT

4 G/0.3 OZ LIQUORICE POWDER

650 G/22 FL OZ/2.7 CUPS WATER

In a saucepan, place the water, chocolate pieces, and cane sugar. Heat, mixing the ingredients together well, adding the carob seed flour, salt and liquorice powder. Bring to 85°C/185°F, keep stirring until the mixture becomes homogenous then rapidly reduce the temperature and place the mixture in the ice cream maker. Work until the right consistency is obtained.

Dark chocolate and rum ice cream

INGREDIENTS

600 G/20.5 FL OZ/2.5 CUPS FRESH WHOLE MILK

80 G/JUST OVER 3 OZ CANE SUGAR

40 G/1.4 FL OZ/0.2 CUPS RUM

2 G/0.1 OZ CAROB SEED FLOUR

150 G/5.1 FL OZ/0.6 CUPS WATER

120 G/JUST UNDER 5 OZ DARK 75% ARRIBA CHOCOLATE

Break up the chocolate and melt in a saucepan with the milk and water. Add the carob seed flour and the cane sugar, mix together well and bring the temperature to 85°C/185°F. Quickly cool the mixture and pour into the ice cream maker. In the creaming phase, when the mixture reaches a temperature of about -5°C/25°F, add the rum and continue to work in the machine until a homogenous creamy ice cream is obtained.

CHOCOLATE
AND COCOA

White chocolate semi-freddo with passion fruit

INGREDIENTS

210 G/JUST OVER 8 OZ WHITE CHOCOLATE

550 G/18.7 FL OZ/2.3 CUPS SEMI-WHIPPED CREAM

FOR THE ITALIAN MERINGUE

45 G/1.5 FL OZ/0.2 CUPS WATER

170 G/JUST UNDER 7 OZ CASTER SUGAR

90 G/JUST UNDER 4 OZ EGG WHITES (ABOUT 2)

FOR THE SAUCE

250 G/10 OZ PASSION FRUIT PULP

120 G/JUST UNDER 1 OZ CASTER SUGAR

10 G/JUST UNDER ½ OZ GELATINE SHEETS

FOR THE BISQUIT

50 G/2 OZ ALMOND FLOUR

15 G/½ OZ HONEY

40 G/JUST UNDER 2 OZ ICING SUGAR

10 G/JUST UNDER ½ OZ POTATO STARCH

100 G/4 OZ EGG WHITES

50 G/2 OZ PISTACHIO NUTS

20 G/0.7 FL OZ/0.1 CUPS CORN OIL

50 G/2 OZ CASTER SUGAR

Prepare the sauce: place the passion fruit and sugar in a pan to cook; bring to 85°C/185°F. Towards the end of the cooking time, add the gelatine, which you have previously hydrated and drained. Remove from the heat and allow to rest. In the meantime, toast the pistachio nuts in a frying pan and whizz them until they turn into a paste (p. 200). Combine the ingredients for the bisquit: blend the almond flour, honey, icing sugar, potato starch, pistachio paste, corn oil and half the egg whites. Whip the other half until stiff and then add the caster sugar. Combine the two mixtures and place in a rectangular mould. Bake in the oven at 180°C/355°F for 12 minutes. Proceed with the preparation of the Italian meringue (p. 204). Melt the white chocolate and gently incorporate it into the meringue, then add the semi-whipped cream. In a mould lined with oven paper, begin to whip the semi-freddo, taking care to cool it in the freezer a few hours after adding/spreading out the sauce. Begin with the bisquit, then the passion fruit, then the meringue mixture. Put another layer of bisquit until you have used all the ingredients.

White chocolate with sugared pistachio nuts and passion fruit

INGREDIENTS

150 G/6 OZ PASSION FRUIT PULP

150 G/6 OZ WHITE CHOCOLATE

140 G/JUST UNDER 6 OZ CASTER SUGAR

600 G/20.5 FL OZ/2.5 CUPS FRESH WHOLE MILK

2 G/0.1 OZ CAROB SEED FLOUR

100 G/4 OZ SHELLED PISTACHIO NUTS

15 G/0.5 FL OZ/0.05 CUPS WATER

———————— ————————

Heat 40 grams/just under 2 oz of sugar with the water and bring to 110°C/230°F. Then add the pistachio nuts, and stir over a medium heat (p. 201). In another saucepan melt the chocolate in the milk and add the passion fruit pulp, sugar and carob seed flour. When the mixture reaches 85°C/185°F, cool rapidly. Pour the mixture into the ice cream maker. When it is ready, add the sugared pistachio nuts and mix well.

Cocoa and orange ice cream

INGREDIENTS

700 G/23.8 FL OZ/JUST UNDER 3 CUPS FRESH WHOLE MILK

200 G/8 OZ CANE SUGAR

THE ZEST OF 2 ORANGES

2 G/0.1 OZ CAROB SEED FLOUR

60 G/JUST OVER 2 OZ COCOA

Pour the sugar into a bowl, add the orange zest and mix well. Place the milk, aromatized sugar, cocoa and carob seed flour in a saucepan over a medium heat; mix well. Use a thermometer to check the temperature: when the mixture reaches 85°C/185°F, remove from the heat and cool quickly. Transfer the mixture to the ice cream maker and work until a perfect consistency has been obtained.

Milk chocolate, toffee and salt ice cream

INGREDIENTS

170 G/5.8 FL OZ/0.7 CUPS TOFFEE SAUCE

120 G/JUST UNDER 5 OZ MILK CHOCOLATE

700 G/23.8 FL OZ/JUST UNDER 3 CUPS FRESH WHOLE MILK

2 G/0.1 OZ CAROB SEED FLOUR

7 G/0.2 OZ SALT

———————————————

Put the milk in a saucepan over a low heat, and begin to warm. Add the broken up chocolate and mix to aid the melting process. Keep stirring then gradually add the carob seed flour, the salt and the toffee sauce (p. 181). Bring to 85°C/185°F. Cool rapidly and place in the ice cream maker; work until the perfect temperature and consistency have been obtained.

fresh
fruit

Lemon and honey granita

Strawberry and mint sorbet

Mango and yogurt sorbet

Pear and clove sorbet

Raspberry semi-freddo

Black cherry sorbet

Black cherry, robiola and balsamic vinegar
ice cream

Apricot and melissa sorbet

Fig and mint sorbet

Bergamot sorbet

Syrupy peach ice cream with hazelnut
and lavender streusel

Persimmon sorbet

Raspberry, rosemary and gin sorbet

Peach and thyme sorbet

Pineapple, rocket and white chocolate ice cream

Strawberry, banana and lime ice cream

Lemon and honey granita

INGREDIENTS

250 G/8.5 FL OZ/1 CUP LEMON JUICE
110 G/JUST OVER 4 OZ HONEY
640 G/21.8 FL OZ/2.7 CUPS WATER

_____ _____

Blend all the ingredients and complete
the preparation in the ice cream maker.

Strawberry and mint sorbet

INGREDIENTS

600 G/1.3 LB STRAWBERRIES
10 SMALL MINT LEAVES

FOR THE SYRUP

220 G/JUST UNDER 9 OZ CASTER SUGAR
2 G/0.1 OZ CAROB SEED FLOUR
180 G/6 FL OZ/0.7 CUPS WATER

Prepare the syrup: place all the ingredients in a saucepan and warm them over a medium heat until they reach 82°C/180°F, stirring from time to time. Cool the syrup.
For the sorbet, blend the strawberries, mint and syrup. Pour the mixture into the ice cream maker and work until the desired consistency is obtained.

INGREDIENTS

200 G/8 OZ MANGO PULP
400 G/13.6 FL OZ/1.7 CUPS YOGURT

FOR THE SYRUP

220 G/JUST UNDER 9 OZ CASTER SUGAR
2 G/0.1 OZ CAROB SEED FLOUR
180 G/6 FL OZ/0.7 CUPS WATER

Prepare the syrup: place all the ingredients in a saucepan and warm them over a medium heat until they reach 82°C/180°F, stirring from time to time. Cool the syrup.

For the sorbet: blend the mango with the yogurt and the syrup until the ingredients are mixed together well. Transfer the mixture to the ice cream maker and proceed. Serve immediately or keep in the freezer.

Mango and yogurt sorbet

Pear and clove sorbet

INGREDIENTS

600 G/1.3 LB ORGANIC OR PEELED PEARS

2 G/0.1 OZ CLOVES

FOR THE SYRUP

220 G/JUST UNDER 9 OZ CASTER SUGAR

2 G/0.1 OZ CAROB SEED FLOUR

180 G/6 FL OZ/0.7 CUPS WATER

After preparing the syrup (p. 97), place it in a large bowl with the chopped pear (if the pear is organic, keep the skin on) and the cloves. Blend well and transfer to the ice cream maker.

FRESH
FRUIT

Raspberry semi-freddo

INGREDIENTS

300 G/10.5 OZ RASPBERRIES

400 G/13.6 FL OZ/1.6 CUPS SEMI-WHIPPED CREAM

FOR THE ITALIAN MERINGUE

60 G/2 FL OZ/0.2 CUPS WATER

240 G/JUST UNDER 10 OZ CASTER SUGAR

120 G/JUST UNDER 9 OZ EGG WHITES (ABOUT 3)

Start by preparing the meringue, combining the water and sugar over the heat. Bring to 110°C/230°F. Whip the egg whites in a food processor, adding the syrup in a fine stream without stopping the machine. Blend the raspberries and add to the meringue. Finally, add the cream and mix carefully.

Place the mixture into individual moulds or one large mould and allow to rest in the freezer overnight.

Black cherry sorbet

INGREDIENTS

500 G/JUST OVER 1 LB PITTED BLACK CHERRIES
100 G/3.4 FL OZ/0.4 CUPS WATER

FOR THE SYRUP

220 G/JUST UNDER 9 OZ CASTER SUGAR
2 G/0.1 OZ CAROB SEED FLOUR
180 G/6 FL OZ/0.7 CUPS WATER

_____ _____

Begin by preparing the syrup (p. 97). Blend the black cherries, water and syrup, to obtain a homogenous purée. Pour the mixture into the ice cream maker and work until a sorbet consistency is obtained. Eat straightaway or keep in the freezer.

Black cherry, robiola and balsamic vinegar ice cream

INGREDIENTS

150 G/6 OZ ROBIOLA CHEESE

300 G/10.5 OZ PITTED BLACK CHERRIES

180 G/JUST OVER 7 OZ CASTER SUGAR

370 G/12.5 FL OZ/1.5 CUPS FRESH WHOLE MILK

2 G/0.1 OZ CAROB SEED FLOUR

A FEW DROPS OF BALSAMIC VINEGAR

―――――――――――― ――――――――――――

Blend all the ingredients: robiola, black cherries, sugar, milk and carob seed flour until the mixture is homogenous. Transfer the mixture to the ice cream maker. Once the desired consistency is obtained, serve, adding a few drops of balsamic vinegar as desired.

Apricot and melissa sorbet

INGREDIENTS

600 G/1.3 LB PITTED APRICOTS
4 G/0.2 OZ MELISSA (ABOUT 10 SMALL LEAVES)

FOR THE SYRUP

220 G/JUST UNDER 9 OZ CASTER SUGAR
2 G/0.1 OZ CAROB SEED FLOUR
180 G/6 FL OZ/0.7 CUPS WATER

————————————————

After preparing the syrup (p. 97), blend all the ingredients and pour into the ice cream maker. Leave to work until the desired consistency is obtained.

fig and mint sorbet

INGREDIENTS

600 G/1.3 LB ORGANIC OR VERY CLEAN FIGS

4 G/0.2 OZ MINT (ABOUT 12 SMALL LEAVES)

  OR 6 G MARJORAM AS AN ALTERNATIVE

  TO MINT

200 G/8 OZ CASTER SUGAR

200 G/6.8 FL OZ/0.8 CUPS WATER

Blend the figs with the mint, sugar and water then transfer the mixture to the ice cream maker and work until the desired consistency is obtained.

Bergamot sorbet

Ingredients

250 G/8.5 FL OZ/1 CUP BERGAMOT JUICE

50 G/2 OZ CASTER SUGAR

300 G/10.2 FL OZ/1.2 CUPS WATER

For the syrup

220 G/JUST UNDER 9 OZ CASTER SUGAR

2 G/0.1 OZ CAROB SEED FLOUR

180 G/6 FL OZ/0.7 CUPS WATER

Prepare the syrup: combine all the ingredients in a saucepan and heat to 82°C/180°F over a medium flame. Stir from time to time then allow to cool.
Blend all the ingredients and pour into the ice cream maker. Work until the desired consistency is obtained.

Syrupy peach ice cream with hazelnut and lavender streusel

FOR THE STREUSEL

150 G/6 OZ COLD BUTTER

150 G/6 OZ HAZELNUT FLOUR

150 G/6 OZ CASTER SUGAR

150 G/6 OZ FLOUR

2 G/0.1 OZ LAVENDER

FOR THE ICE CREAM

100 G/3.4 FL OZ/0.4 CUPS CREAM

300 G/12 OZ PEACHES IN SYRUP

180 G/JUST OVER 7 OZ CASTER SUGAR

420 G/14.2 FL OZ/1.8 CUPS FRESH
  WHOLE MILK

2 G/0.1 OZ CAROB SEED FLOUR

Place the chopped butter in a container with all the streusel ingredients and mix with a spoon until a granular homogenous mixture is obtained. Remember that lavender has a very characteristic aroma: if you prefer a more delicate flavour, lower the dose. Spread the mixture on a baking tray lined with oven paper and bake in the oven at 180°C/355°F for 25-30 minutes. Allow to cool. In the meantime, prepare the ice cream: warm the milk, add the sugar, carob seed flour, cream and the pieces of syrupy peaches. Remove from the heat before the temperature exceeds 85°C/185°F and pour the mixture into the ice cream maker. At the end of the process, add the streusel as desired, mix well and serve.

Persimmon sorbet

Ingredients

400 g/**14** oz clean persimmons

220 g/just under **9** oz caster sugar

400 g/**13.6** fl oz/**1.7** cups water

_____ _____

Blend the persimmons, sugar and water. Transfer the mixture to the ice cream maker and work until the desired consistency is obtained. Serve straightaway or keep in the freezer.

FRESH
FRUIT

Raspberry, rosemary and gin sorbet

INGREDIENTS

500 G/JUST OVER 1 LB RASPBERRIES

2 G/0.1 OZ ROSEMARY

180 G/JUST OVER 7 OZ CASTER SUGAR

275 G/9.3 FL OZ/1.1 CUPS WATER

40 G/1.3 FL OZ/0.15 CUPS GIN

2 G/0.1 OZ CAROB SEED FLOUR

_____ _____

Blend all the ingredients until the mixture
is creamy. Pour it into the ice cream maker
and work until the sorbet is ready.

Peach and thyme sorbet

FRESH FRUIT

INGREDIENTS

600 G/1.3 LB ORGANIC PEACHES
5 G/0.2 OZ THYME

FOR THE SYRUP

220 G/JUST UNDER 7 OZ CASTER SUGAR
2 G/0.1 OZ CAROB SEED FLOUR
180 G/6 FL OZ/0.7 CUPS WATER

——————————— ———————————

Prepare the syrup: combine all the ingredients in a saucepan and warm over a medium heat until the mixture reaches 82°C/180°F, stirring from time to time. Allow to cool.
Blend the peaches, thyme and syrup until the mixture is homogenous. Pour it into the ice cream maker and work until a sorbet consistency is obtained.

Pineapple, rocket and white chocolate ice cream

INGREDIENTS

150 G/6 OZ WHITE CHOCOLATE

300 G/10.5 OZ CLEAN PINEAPPLE

100 G/4 OZ CASTER SUGAR

10 G/0.3 OZ ROCKET

450 G/15.3 FL OZ/1.8 CUPS FRESH WHOLE MILK

2 G/0.1 OZ CAROB SEED FLOUR

Blend the rocket and pineapple in a bowl until it resembles a purée. Warm the milk and add the white chocolate, which you have previously broken into small pieces. Stir to melt the chocolate, add the sugar and the carob seed flour. Cook at 85°C/185°F then cool the mixture rapidly. Add the pineapple and rocket purée before placing the mixture in the ice cream maker to complete the preparation.

Strawberry, banana and lime ice cream

INGREDIENTS

100 G/3.4 FL OZ/0.4 CUPS CREAM

200 G/8 OZ STRAWBERRIES

150 G/6 OZ BANANA PULP

THE ZEST OF 1 LIME

180 G/JUST OVER 7 OZ CASTER SUGAR

370 G/12.5 FL OZ/1.5 CUPS FRESH WHOLE MILK

2 G/0.1 OZ CAROB SEED FLOUR

Put the chopped strawberries and bananas in a bowl and blend with an immersion blender. Place the milk, cream, sugar and carob seed flour into a saucepan over a medium heat; during the whole cooking time the temperature should reach 85°C/185°F. Allow to cool then add the lime zest and the blended fruit. Continue to stir. When it is well-blended, transfer to the ice cream maker to finish the preparation.

nuts

SALTED ALMOND AND VANILLA ICE CREAM

HAZELNUT ICE CREAM

BACIO SORBET

CREMINO ICE CREAM

ALMOND AND CINNAMON GRANITA

PINE NUT AND WHITE CARDAMOM ICE CREAM

PISTACHIO, MANDARIN JUICE AND STAR ANISE SORBET

PISTACHIO ICE CREAM

Salted almond and vanilla ice cream

INGREDIENTS

100 G/4 OZ ALMONDS

1 VANILLA POD

5 G/0.2 OZ SALT

170 G/JUST UNDER **7** OZ CASTER SUGAR

20 G/JUST UNDER **1** OZ EGG YOLK (ABOUT **1**)

700 G/23.8 FL OZ/2.9 CUPS FRESH WHOLE MILK

2 G/0.1 OZ CAROB SEED FLOUR

Roughly chop the almonds. Mix the egg yolk and beat with a whisk, adding the milk. Place over a medium heat. Add the salt, sugar, carob seed flour and almonds; cook. Keep an eye on the temperature with a cooking thermometer: when the temperature reaches 82°C/180°F, add the vanilla pod and leave to infuse for a few minutes. When the mixture reaches 85°C/185°F, remove the pod and allow the mixture to cool. Once cold, pour into the ice cream maker and work.

Hazelnut ice cream

INGREDIENTS

100 G/4 OZ HAZELNUTS

200 G/8 OZ CASTER SUGAR

20 G/JUST UNDER 1 OZ EGG YOLK (ABOUT 1)

700 G/23.8 FL OZ/2.9 CUPS FRESH WHOLE MILK

2 G/0.1 OZ CAROB SEED FLOUR

———————— ————————

Toast the hazelnuts and chop them roughly if you wish the ice cream to have a crunch, or keep chopping until you have a fine paste. Beat the egg yolk with a whisk then add the milk. Place a saucepan over a medium heat and gradually add the other ingredients, bringing the mixture to 85°C/185°F. If you prefer a creamier ice cream, substitute 60 g/just over 2 fl oz/0.2 cups of milk with 60 g/just over 2 oz of egg yolk. Cool the mixture rapidly before pouring into the ice cream maker.

Bacio sorbet

INGREDIENTS

40 G/JUST UNDER 2 OZ COCOA

160 G/JUST OVER 6 OZ HAZELNUTS

250 G/10 OZ CASTER SUGAR

2 G/0.1 OZ CAROB SEED FLOUR

660 G/22.4 FL OZ/2.7 CUPS WATER

Toast 60 g/just over 2 oz of hazelnuts and chop them finely. Place the water, cocoa, sugar and carob seed flour into a saucepan. Stir over the heat and bring the temperature to 85°C/185°F. Once the mixture is homogenous, remove from the heat and cool rapidly. Add the chopped hazelnuts and pour the mixture into the ice cream maker. Once the ice cream is ready, add whole hazelnuts and mix well. Keep in the freezer or serve immediately.

Cremino ice cream

50 G/2 OZ HAZELNUTS

100 G/4 OZ WHITE CHOCOLATE

160 G/JUST OVER 6 OZ CASTER SUGAR

2 G/0.1 OZ CAROB SEED FLOUR

700 G/23.8 FL OZ/2.9 CUPS FRESH WHOLE MILK

Toast the hazelnuts and blend them until they turn into a paste (p. 200). Warm the milk and, stirring continuously, add the chocolate; allow to melt. Combine the other ingredients: the sugar, carob seed flour and the hazelnut paste. The mixture must not reach boiling point; once the temperature has reached 85°C/185°F, allow to cool and pour the mixture into the ice cream maker.

NUTS

NUTS

Almond and cinnamon granita

INGREDIENTS

100 G/4 OZ ALMONDS

150 G/6 OZ CASTER SUGAR

5 G/0.2 OZ CINNAMON

750 G/25.5 FL OZ/3.1 CUPS WATER

Toast the almonds then blend them to create a paste (p. 200). Place the water, almond paste, sugar and cinnamon in a saucepan over the heat, stirring well. Use a thermometer to check that the temperature of the mixture reaches 85°C/185°F, then remove from the heat and cool rapidly. Work the mixture in the ice cream maker then serve.

Pine nut and white cardamom ice cream

INGREDIENTS

100 G/4 OZ PINE NUTS

5 WHITE CARDAMOM PODS

200 G/8 OZ CASTER SUGAR

700 G/23.8 FL OZ/2.9 CUPS FRESH WHOLE MILK

2 G/0.1 OZ CAROB SEED FLOUR

———————————— ————————————

Toast the pine nuts and blend them until
a paste is obtained (p. 200). Grind the
cardamom pods and mix with the sugar.
In the meantime, place the milk and all
the other ingredients in a saucepan over a
medium heat. Add the cardamom sugar, mix
and cook at 85°C/185°F. Allow to cool then
work in the ice cream maker.

Pistachio, mandarin juice and star anise sorbet

INGREDIENTS

100 G/4 OZ PISTACHIO NUTS

400 G/13.6 FL OZ/1.6 CUPS MANDARIN JUICE

180 G/JUST OVER 7 OZ CASTER SUGAR

2 G/0.1 OZ CAROB SEED FLOUR

1 STAR ANISE

300 G/10.2 FL OZ/1.2 CUPS WATER

————————————— —————————————

Begin by toasting and chopping the pistachio nuts to create a paste (p. 200). Heat the water, sugar, carob seed flour, star anise, mandarin juice and pistachio paste in a saucepan. Keep stirring and check the temperature: when the mixture reaches 85°C/185°F, remove from the heat, cool and work in the ice cream maker.

Pistachio ice cream

100 G/**4** OZ PISTACHIO NUTS

200 G/**8** OZ CASTER SUGAR

700 G/**23.8** FL OZ/**2.9** CUPS FRESH WHOLE MILK

2 G/**0.1** OZ CAROB SEED FLOUR

Toast and chop the pistachio nuts to form a paste (p. 200). Place the milk, sugar, carob seed flour and pistachio paste in a pan over a low heat, without the mixture reaching boiling point. When 85°C/185°F is reached, remove the pan from the heat, allow the mixture to cool and pour it into the ice cream maker to obtain a homogenous, creamy ice cream.

sweet baking
in ice cream

STRUDEL ICE CREAM

PANETTONE ICE CREAM

CASSATA ICE CREAM

SICILIAN CANNOLO ICE CREAM

GRANNY'S JAM TART ICE CREAM

CARROT CAKE ICE CREAM

CHOCOLATE CAKE ICE CREAM

BREAD, BUTTER AND JAM ICE CREAM

COOKIE ICE CREAM

TIRAMISÙ ICE CREAM

RUM BABA ICE CREAM

NEAPOLITAN PASTIERA ICE CREAM

CHEESECAKE ICE CREAM

Strudel ice cream

INGREDIENTS

100 G/4 OZ EGG YOLKS (ABOUT 5)

620 G/21 FL OZ/2.6 CUPS FRESH WHOLE MILK

180 G/JUST OVER 7 OZ CASTER SUGAR

2 G/0.1 OZ CAROB SEED FLOUR

40 G/JUST UNDER 2 OZ PINE NUTS

40 G/JUST UNDER 2 OZ SULTANAS

50 G/2 OZ COOKED SHORTCRUST PASTRY

100 G/3.4 FL OZ/0.4 CUPS APPLE SAUCE (P. 179)

———————————— ————————————

Mix the egg yolks and the sugar with a whisk, to obtain a foamy mixture. Warm the milk in a saucepan, add the foamy mixture and the carob seed flour. Leave to cook, bring to 85°C/185°F then cool quickly and place the mixture in the ice cream maker. At this point, you can choose to variegate with the apple sauce, pine nuts, sultanas and shortcrust pastry, or add a portion of ready-made strudel which you have previously blended.

Panettone ice cream

INGREDIENTS

670 G/22.7 FL OZ/2.8 CUPS FRESH WHOLE MILK

60 G/2 FL OZ/0.2 CUPS CREAM

60 G/JUST OVER 2 OZ EGG YOLKS (ABOUT 3)

200 G/8 OZ CASTER SUGAR

2 G/0.1 OZ CAROB SEED FLOUR

150 G/6 OZ PANETTONE

_____ _____

Blend the panettone in a mixer and put aside. Combine the egg yolks with the sugar and beat with a whisk until a foamy mixture is obtained. Pour the mixture in a small pan with the milk, cream and the carob seed flour. Place on a low heat and stir as you turn the heat up to moderate. Bring the temperature of the mixture up to 85°C/185°F; when the mixture is well-combined, remove from the heat. Cool rapidly and transfer to the ice cream maker to complete the process. Add the blended panettone and mix well.

Cassata ice cream

150 G/6 OZ MIXED (GOAT'S AND COW'S MILK) RICOTTA CHEESE

20 G/JUST UNDER 1 OZ ALMONDS

180 G/JUST OVER 7 OZ CASTER SUGAR

650 G/22 FL OZ/2.7 CUPS FRESH WHOLE MILK

2 G/0.1 OZ CAROB SEED FLOUR

100 G/4 OZ DARK CHOCOLATE

40 G/0.2 OZ CANDIED FRUIT

——————————— ———————————

Toast and blend the almonds to form a paste (p. 200). Warm the milk, ricotta, almond paste, sugar and carob seed flour, stirring all the time: the mixture needs to reach 85°C/185°F and be well-mixed. Then remove from the heat, cool quickly and work in the ice cream maker. Right at the end, add the chocolate shavings and candied fruit.

Sicilian cannolo ice cream

150 g/6 oz sheep's milk ricotta cheese

180 g/just over 7 oz caster sugar

680 g/23.1 fl oz/2.8 cups fresh whole milk

2 g/0.1 oz carob seed flour

1 cannolo tube

_____ _____

Crush the cannolo tube into pieces and put aside. Place the milk, ricotta, sugar and carob seed flour into a saucepan and mix well. Measure the temperature; once it has reached 85°C/185°F, remove from the heat and cool rapidly. Transfer the mixture to the ice cream maker and complete the process. When it is ready, add the pieces of cannolo cone.

Granny's jam tart ice cream

INGREDIENTS

80 G/JUST OVER 3 OZ EGG YOLKS (ABOUT 4)

120 G/JUST UNDER 5 OZ CREAM

200 G/8 OZ CASTER SUGAR

600 G/20.5 FL OZ/2.5 CUPS FRESH WHOLE MILK

2 G/0.1 OZ CAROB SEED FLOUR

150 G/6 OZ GRANNY'S JAM TART BROKEN
  INTO PIECES (P. 209)

Beat the egg yolks and the sugar together in a saucepan until the mixture foams. Add the milk, cream and carob seed flour. Bring to 85°C/185°F, then cool quickly. Pour the mixture into the ice cream maker and work until the desired consistency is obtained. When it is ready, add the pieces of jam tart.

Carrot cake
ice cream

INGREDIENTS

730 G/24.8 FL OZ/3 CUPS FRESH WHOLE MILK

70 G/JUST UNDER 3 OZ MASCARPONE CHEESE

190 G/JUST UNDER 8 OZ CASTER SUGAR

2 G/0.1 OZ CAROB SEED FLOUR

200 G/8 OZ CARROT CAKE (P. 211)

——————————— ———————————

Chop the carrot cake in a mixer and put aside. Warm the milk with the mascarpone, sugar and the carob seed flour. Measure the temperature with a thermometer: when the mixture reaches 85°C/185°F, remove from the heat and cool quickly. Place in the ice cream maker and work the mixture. Only when the ice cream is ready, add the carrot cake.

Chocolate cake ice cream

INGREDIENTS

700 G/23.8 FL OZ/2.9 CUPS FRESH WHOLE MILK

60 G/JUST OVER 2 OZ MASCARPONE CHEESE

20 G/JUST UNDER 1 OZ EGG YOLK (ABOUT 1)

200 G/8 OZ CASTER SUGAR

2 G/0.1 OZ CAROB SEED FLOUR

200 G/8 OZ CHOCOLATE CAKE (P. 210)

_____ _____

Blend the chocolate cake until a fine paste is obtained. Beat the sugar and egg yolk in a bowl with a whisk. Place the milk, mascarpone, sugar mixture and carob seed flour into a saucepan over a medium heat and warm. Heat until the temperature of the mixture reaches 85°C/185°F. Cool quickly before placing in the ice cream maker. Once ready, mix in the cake paste.

Bread, butter and jam ice cream

INGREDIENTS

50 G/2 OZ BUTTER

750 G/25.5 FL OZ/3.1 CUPS FRESH WHOLE MILK

200 G/8 OZ CASTER SUGAR

2 G/0.1 OZ CAROB SEED FLOUR

100 G/3.4 FL OZ/0.4 CUPS BLACK CHERRY SAUCE (P. 187)

70 G/JUST UNDER 3 OZ BRIOCHE BUN

—————————— ——————————

Warm the milk, butter, sugar and the carob seed flour in a saucepan, taking care to stir until the mixture reaches 85°C/185°F. Cool quickly and place in the ice cream maker. Finally, add a few spoonfuls of black cherry sauce and the brioche bun in crumbs.

Cookie ice cream

INGREDIENTS

80 g/just over **3** oz egg yolks (about **4**)

110 g/3.7 fl oz/0.4 cups cream

200 g/8 oz caster sugar

600 g/20.5 fl oz/2.5 cups fresh whole milk

2 g/0.1 oz carob seed flour

100 g/4 oz cookies (p. 212)

———————————— ————————————

Beat the egg yolks with the sugar until the mixture becomes foamy, then add the milk, cream and carob seed flour. Warm over a medium heat and check with a thermometer that the temperature reaches 85°C/185°F: remove from the heat and cool rapidly before transferring the mixture to the ice cream maker. Finally, add the cookies, which you have broken into pieces, and mix well.

For the ice cream

150 G/6 OZ MASCARPONE CHEESE

60 G/JUST OVER 2 OZ EGG YOLKS
(ABOUT 3)

2 G/0.1 OZ CAROB SEED FLOUR

210 G/JUST OVER 8 OZ CASTER SUGAR

5-6 SAVOIARDI (LADYFINGER) BISCUITS

COCOA POWDER FOR DUSTING

For the coffee infusion

660 G/22.4 FL OZ/2.7 CUPS MILK

80 G/JUST OVER 3 OZ COARSELY
GROUND OR MOKA COFFEE
GRANULES

Prepare the infusion of coffee and milk: warm the milk until boiling point. Pour in the freshly ground coffee and leave to infuse for 4 or 5 minutes, then filter.

In a bowl, beat the egg yolks and sugar with a whisk until the mixture foams. Warm the infusion in a saucepan with the foamy mixture, the mascarpone and the carob seed flour. Bring to 85°C/185°F then remove from the heat, cool rapidly before placing in the ice cream maker. Finally, add the tiny pieces of savoiardi biscuits and mix well. Dust with cocoa powder.

Tiramisù
ice cream

Rum baba ice cream

INGREDIENTS

100 g/4 oz egg yolks (about 5)
125 g/4.2 fl oz/0.5 cups cream
200 g/8 oz caster sugar
580 g/19.7 fl oz/2.4 cups fresh whole milk
150 g/6 oz rum babas

In a large bowl, beat the egg yolks with the sugar until the mixture is foamy. Place the milk in a saucepan and turn on the heat. Combine the cream and the egg yolk mixture in the pan and stir. Using a thermometer to help you, check that the mixture reaches 85°C/185°F, remove from the heat and cool quickly. The mixture can then be placed in the ice cream maker and the process completed. Finally, add the rum babas which you have previously chopped finely.

Neapolitan pastiera ice cream

For the pastiera sauce

200 g/8 oz cooked wheat

100 g/3.4 fl oz/0.4 cups cream

50 g/2 oz honey

2 drops of orange flower essential oil

For the ice cream

100 g/4 oz egg yolks (about 5)

110 g/just over 4 oz caster sugar

400 g/13.6 fl oz/1.6 cups fresh whole milk

100 g/4 oz ricotta cheese

100 g/4 oz puff pastry

The zest of 1 orange

Prepare the pastiera sauce: cook the wheat with the cream in a saucepan until a creamy sauce is obtained, then add the honey and cook for a minute or two. Add the drops of orange flower essential oil and continue to stir carefully. Put aside.

In the mixer, blend a few pieces of puff pastry and put aside. Beat the egg yolks and gradually add the other ingredients (sugar, milk and ricotta) in a pan over a medium heat.

Cook and bring the mixture to 85°C/185°F. Add the orange zest to enrich the ice cream with aromatic notes.

Cool quickly and place the mixture in the ice cream maker. When the ice cream is ready, add the small pieces of puff pastry and mix well.

Cheesecake ice cream

150 g/6 oz robiola cheese

20 g/just under 1 oz egg yolk (about 1)

200 g/8 oz caster sugar

630 g/21.4 fl oz/2.6 cups fresh whole milk

100 g/3.4 fl oz/0.4 cups blueberry sauce

80 g/just over 3 oz puff pastry

———————— ————————

Blend the robiola, sugar, milk and egg yolk, stirring continuously until the mixture reaches 85°C/185°F. Cool quickly and use the ice cream maker to complete the preparation. At the end, add the blueberry sauce and some pieces of puff pastry.

For a really tasty snack, you could fill some sweet mini focaccias (p. 213) with this ice cream.

gourmet ice cream

——————— ———————

BUTTER AND ANCHOVY ICE CREAM

FONTINA, ORANGE ZEST, OVEN-BAKED BLACK OLIVE
AND FENNEL SEED ICE CREAM

CREAMED HERB SALTED COD ICE CREAM

GORGONZOLA AND PEPPER ICE CREAM

——————— ———————

Butter and anchovy ice cream

INGREDIENTS

100 G/4 OZ TREHALOSE

50 G/2 OZ DEXTROSE

70 G/JUST UNDER 3 OZ POWDERED SKIMMED MILK

50 G/2 OZ BUTTER

100 G/4 OZ ANCHOVIES

10 G/JUST UNDER ½ OZ SALT

2 G/0.1 OZ CAROB SEED FLOUR

620 G/21 FL OZ/2.6 CUPS WATER

_____ _____

Place all the ingredients in a saucepan except the anchovies and butter. Bring the mixture to 85°C/185°F. Once this temperature has been reached, remove from the heat and add the butter, mixing until it has completely melted. Cool the mixture, add the anchovies and blend. When the mixture is homogenous, you can transfer it to the ice cream maker.

INGREDIENTS

3 OR 4 OVEN-BAKED BLACK OLIVES

200 G/8 OZ FONTINA CHEESE

50 G/2 OZ SKIMMED MILK POWDER

100 G/4 OZ TREHALOSE

50 G/2 OZ DEXTROSE

7 G/0.2 OZ SALT

2 G/0.1 OZ CAROB SEED FLOUR

600 G/20.5 FL OZ/2.5 CUPS WATER

4 OR 5 FENNEL SEEDS

THE ZEST OF ½ AN ORANGE

———————————— ————————————

Remove the stones of the oven-baked olives and chop them finely. Heat the water then add the fontina, milk, trehalose, dextrose, salt and carob seed flour. Mix well: the mixture must be homogenous. Add the fennel seeds, olives and orange zest to enrich the mixture with aromatic notes. When the thermometer reads 85°C/185°F, remove the mixture from the heat and cool rapidly. Place in the ice cream maker.

fontina, orange zest, oven-baked black olive and fennel seed ice cream

Creamed herb salted cod ice cream

250 G/10 OZ SALTED COD

70 G/JUST UNDER 3 OZ SKIMMED MILK POWDER

100 G/4 OZ TREHALOSE

50 G/2 OZ DEXTROSE

7 G/0.2 OZ SALT

2 G/0.1 OZ CAROB SEED FLOUR

520 G/17.7 FL OZ/2.2 CUPS WATER

20 G/JUST UNDER 1 OZ EXTRA-VIRGIN OLIVE OIL

2 G/0.1 OZ THYME

1 G/A PINCH OF MARJORAM

THE ZEST OF ½ A LEMON

——————————— ———————————

Blend the salted cod. Put the water in a pan to heat and gradually add the milk, trehalose, dextrose, salted cod, salt and the carob seed flour. Keep stirring and bring to 85°C/185°F. Add the thyme and marjoram. For a more complex and fresh flavour, you can add the lemon zest during cooking time. Finally, just before creaming, add the cold extra-virgin olive oil. Allow the mixture to cool before working in the ice cream maker.

Gorgonzola and pepper ice cream

INGREDIENTS

150 G/6 OZ GRILLED PEPPERS

200 G/8 OZ GORGONZOLA CHEESE

50 G/2 OZ SKIMMED MILK POWDER

100 G/4 OZ TREHALOSE

50 G/2 OZ DEXTROSE

7 G/0.2 OZ SALT

2 G/0.1 OZ CAROB SEED FLOUR

440 G/14.9 FL OZ/1.8 CUPS WATER

———————————— ————————————

Chop the peppers in the mixer. Place the water in a pan to heat and add, one at a time, all the ingredients, taking care to mix well. Once the mixture is homogenous and has reached 85°C/185°F, remove from the heat and cool rapidly. Finally, complete the preparation in the ice cream maker.

variegations

RASPBERRY SAUCE

APPLE SAUCE

TOFFEE SAUCE

CARAMEL SAUCE

FRUITS OF THE FOREST SAUCE

BLACK CHERRY SAUCE

PEAR SAUCE

COCOA SAUCE

ORANGE SAUCE

FIG SAUCE

Raspberry sauce

INGREDIENTS

330 G/11.5 OZ RASPBERRIES
120 G/JUST UNDER 5 OZ CASTER SUGAR
2 G/0.1 OZ CAROB SEED FLOUR

_____ _____

Combine the fresh raspberries, sugar and the carob seed flour in a saucepan; bring to the boil, stirring regularly. Leave to cook for about two minutes, then remove from the heat and leave the mixture to cool. Blend in the mixer to obtain a homogenous consistency. It will keep in the fridge for 4 or 5 days.

Apple sauce

INGREDIENTS

350 G/14 OZ APPLE PULP

250 G/10 OZ CASTER SUGAR

2 G/0.1 OZ CAROB SEED FLOUR

10 G/0.3 FL OZ LEMON JUICE

After blending the apples to a homogenous pulp, combine all the ingredients and place them in a pan to cook until the mixture reaches 85°C/185°F. Remember to stir often, so that the mixture is well combined. Allow to cool. Keep in the fridge and consume within 4 or 5 days of preparation.

Toffee sauce

200 G/8 OZ CASTER SUGAR

70 G/JUST UNDER 3 OZ CREAM

90 G/3 FL OZ/0.3 CUPS FRESH
   WHOLE MILK

Caramelize the sugar dry in a heavy-based saucepan, until it turns a blonde colour. In the meantime, warm the milk and cream. Then add the milk and cream mixture in a very slow, fine stream to the sugar, making sure the mixture is very hot. Stir until the mixture is well combined. Allow to cool then keep in the fridge.

Caramel sauce

INGREDIENTS

500 G/1.1 LB CASTER SUGAR
250 G/8.5 FL OZ/1 CUP WATER

_____ _____

Caramelize the sugar dry in a heavy-based pan until it turns a blonde colour. In another saucepan, bring the water to the boil and when the sugar is caramelized, add the water very slowly, stirring carefully.

200 G/8 OZ BLUEBERRIES

100 G/4 OZ RASPBERRIES

50 G/2 OZ PITTED BLACK CHERRIES

50 G/2 OZ BLACKBERRIES

150 G/6 OZ CASTER SUGAR

3 G/0.15 OZ CAROB SEED FLOUR

_____ _____

Place all the fruits in a saucepan over the heat, combine with the sugar and the carob seed flour. Bring to the boil. Cook for two minutes over a moderate heat. When the mixture is homogenous, leave it to cool. Consume within 4 or 5 days of preparation.

fruits of the forest sauce

Black cherry sauce

350 G/14 OZ PITTED BLACK CHERRIES
130 G/JUST OVER 5 OZ CASTER SUGAR
2 G/0.1 OZ CAROB SEED FLOUR

_____ _____

Combine the pitted black cherries, sugar and carob seed flour in a saucepan and cook over a medium heat. Bring to the boil and leave to boil for about two minutes, stirring to mix the ingredients well. Allow to cool and keep in the fridge for no more than 5 days.

Pear sauce

350 g/14 oz pear pulp

250 g/10 oz caster sugar

2 g/0.1 oz carob seed flour

10 g/0.3 fl oz/a few drops lemon juice

Combine all the ingredients and heat, bringing the temperature of the mixture to 85°C/185°F. Stir now and again, then allow to cool and use to variegate your ice cream. This sauce can be kept in the fridge for a maximum of 5 days.

VARIEG
ATIONS

Cocoa sauce

INGREDIENTS

100 g/4 oz cocoa

300 g/12 oz caster sugar

4 g/0.2 oz carob seed flour

600 g/20.5 fl oz/2.5 cups water

——————————— ———————————

Place the water, sugar and cocoa in
a saucepan and heat. Stir until the
ingredients have melted completely, then
add the carob seed flour. Continue to cook,
bringing the temperature to 95°C/200°F,
then allow to cool and keep in the fridge.

VARIEG ATIONS

Orange sauce

INGREDIENTS

500 G/1.1 LB CLEAN ORANGES
350 G/14 OZ SUGAR

_____ _____

Boil a large pan of water and peel the oranges. When the water starts to boil, add the whole oranges and leave to cook for about 40 minutes. Then cut the oranges and remove the pips. Add the sugar and blend the mixture, continuing to cook until you have the desired consistency.

fig sauce

INGREDIENTS

500 G/1.1 LB FIG PIECES

200 G/8 OZ CASTER SUGAR

100 G/4 OZ WATER

10 G/0.3 FL OZ/A FEW DROPS LEMON JUICE

———————————— ————————————

Heat the water and dissolve the sugar. Then add the figs and lemon juice. Continue stirring over a low heat until you have the desired consistency. This sauce can be kept in the fridge for a maximum of 4 or 5 days.

how
to...

How to make nut paste

How to make praline/sugared fruits

How to make nut brittle

How to make Italian meringue

How to know when ice cream or granita is ready

How to cool a mixture or a sugar syrup

How to make nut paste

Toast the nuts for a minute or two in a non-stick frying pan until golden. Place in a blender and work until a homogenous fine-grained mixture is obtained.

How to make praline/sugared fruits

Place the sugar and water in a saucepan,
warm over a medium heat and bring
the temperature to 110°C/230°F. Add
the fruits and stir until all the water has
evaporated. When the sugar starts to stick
to the fruit, remove from the heat and
continue mixing.

How to make nut brittle

Place the sugar in a saucepan over a low heat and caramelize dry until it becomes a blonde colour. Heat the nuts in the oven at 120°C/250°F for about 7 minutes and add the sugar; stir to obtain a homogenous mixture. Add a knob of butter to loosen the caramel from the frying pan then spread it over oven paper, with the help of a lemon.

HOW TO MAKE ITALIAN MERINGUE

Place the water and sugar in a saucepan over a medium heat and bring to 110°C/230°F. In the meantime, whip the egg whites in a blender until stiff. When the sugar syrup reaches 121°C/250°F, pour it in a stream over the egg whites, keeping the mixer running at its highest speed.
Leave the mixer running until the meringue is cool.

How to know when ice cream or granita is ready

Ice cream is ready when the surface results in a homogenous and plastic appearance. Granita is ready when its surface appears rippled and it begins to look plastic.

How to cool a mixture or a sugar syrup

Place some ice in a bowl, pour the hot mixture into a smaller bowl. Immerse the latter in the ice and mix now and again.

sweet
baking

Granny's jam tart

300 g/12 oz all purpose type "00" flour

150 g/6 oz butter

80 g/just over 3 oz caster sugar

60 g/just over 2 oz egg yolks (about 3)

A pinch of salt

400 g/14 oz apricot jam

Mix the flour with the sugar and salt, add the butter in pieces and the egg yolks. Work until you have a compact and uniform dough. Use a rolling pin to roll out the pastry between two sheets of oven paper, to a width of about half a centimetre, taking care to leave a piece for the strips across the top. Line a mould 22 centimetres/8.5 inches in diameter and place it in the freezer for about 10 minutes.

Bake the pastry case in the oven at 180°C/350°F (taking it directly from the freezer to the oven), cook for about half an hour (it should be a blonde colour and almost cooked). Remove from the oven and cover with apricot jam. Make a grill pattern with the remaining pastry and finish the cooking (it will take another ten minutes).

Chocolate cake

100 g/4 oz butter

80 g/just over 3 oz dark chocolate - 55%

40 g/1.5 oz egg yolks (about 2)

100 g/4 oz caster sugar

60 g/2.5 oz egg whites

20 g/just under 1 oz potato starch

20 g/just under 1 oz bitter cocoa

Work the butter to make it creamy then combine with the melted chocolate. Whip the egg yolks with 40 g/1.5 oz of sugar, the sifted potato starch and the cocoa. Whip the egg whites until stiff with the rest of the sugar and incorporate them in the mixture. Place the mixture in the oven at 180°C/350°F and bake for 30-35 minutes.

Carrot cake

350 g/14 oz grated carrots

350 g/11.9 fl oz/1.4 cups sunflower oil

10 g/0.3 oz bicarbonate of soda

6 whole eggs

350 g/14 oz caster sugar

300 g/12 oz all purpose type "00" flour

15 g/just over ½ oz baking powder for sweet recipes

5 g/0.3 oz cinnamon

Beat the eggs with the sugar using a mixer. Add the sunflower oil in a fine stream followed by the flour, bicarbonate of soda, baking powder, cinnamon and grated carrots. Make the mixture homogenous, pour into a baking tray and cook in the oven at 180°C/350°F for 50 minutes.

Cookies

200 g/8 oz soft butter

250 g/10 oz cane sugar

80 g/just over 3 oz whole eggs

300 g/12 oz flour

5 g/0.2 oz bicarbonate of soda

2 g/0.1 oz baking powder for sweet recipes

150 g/6 oz chocolate shavings

Mix the butter with the sugar and work the mixture at room temperature. Add the eggs and mix. Sift the flour, bicarbonate of soda and the baking powder then add them to the mixture. Add the chocolate last. When the mixture is homogenous, form lines of dough and place in the fridge for a couple of hours. Cut the lines into cookies about half a centimetre /0.2 inches thick, place them on a baking tray and bake in the oven at 170°C/335°F for 16 minutes.

Sweet mini focaccia

500 g/17 fl oz/2.1 cups fresh whole milk

40 g/1.5 oz baker's yeast

170 g/just under 7 oz caster sugar

20 g/just under 1 oz salt

200 g/8 oz whole eggs

1 kg/2.2 lb type "00" wheat flour

250 g/10 oz butter

Prepare the poolish: in a bowl large enough to contain the mixture once risen (the volume should triple), melt the yeast in the milk, add 500 g/1.1 lb of flour, 2 g/0.1 oz of sugar and mix. Cover with cling film and place in a warm position until the volume triples.

Place the poolish in a mixing machine with the flour, remaining sugar and the eggs. Work for about 15 minutes until a smooth stringy dough is obtained. Add the salt and the soft butter; allow the dough to absorb these. Remove the dough from the mixer and place in a bowl, cover with cling film and leave to rise at room temperature for about an hour and a half. Next, place the covered dough in the fridge for at least 12 hours. After this time, remove the dough from the fridge, form balls of about 100 g/4 oz, leave to rise at 27°C/87°F for 2 and a half hours. Bake at 180°C/350°F for 15-20 minutes.

index

general index

Acknowledgments

Gimmo, thank you for your support and patience.
Cristiano, thank you for giving me my first real ice cream maker.
Martina, thank you for your precious work.
Giacinto, thank you for having lent me your collection of ice cream scoops.
Cinzia, thank you for your love of markets.
Thanks to Benedetta and Paola, you have been irreplaceable work companions.
Thank you, Simone. With your ice creams you have made me put on several pounds.

Lydia

Thank you...
to Monica, Niccolò and Penelope: for illuminating my days.
To my parents for having given me an inquiring mind.
To Arianna Gandolfi and Cristina Scateni for their support and because I have such fun working with them.
To Lydia for having believed in me and given me this wonderful opportunity.
To "Gelatiere Musso" for their helpfulness.
To Gianfrancesco Cutelli, Carmela Grotta, Andrea Soban, Paolo Brunelli, Stefano Guizzetti, Simone Padoan, Leonardo Di Carlo, Antonio Mezzalira, Antonio Luzi, Alberto Marchetti, Andrea Incerti Vezzani, Giovanna Musumeci, Nicolò Scaglione, Andrea "Strabba" Tamagnini, Tullio Bondi, Raffaele Del Verme, Andrea Bandiera, Mirko Tognetti, Matteo Carloni, Giovanni Giberti, Renato Romano, Matteo Pastorino, the Galliera Boyz, Alessandro Trezza, Angelo Grasso, Alessandro Belli and many other friends with whom I share so much and who help me to grow, showing me the way with passion, dedication and a touch of craziness.
To Matteo Razzini, for his patience, irony and the ability to improvise.

Simone

© Guido Tommasi Editore – Datanova S.r.l., 2019

Text: Lydia Capasso, Simone De Feo
Photographs: Benedetta Marchi
Postproduction: Paola Di Virgilio
Graphics: Carolina Quaresima
Translation: Lucy Howell
Editing: Anita Ravasio

ISBN: 978 88 6753 249 0

Printed in Italy

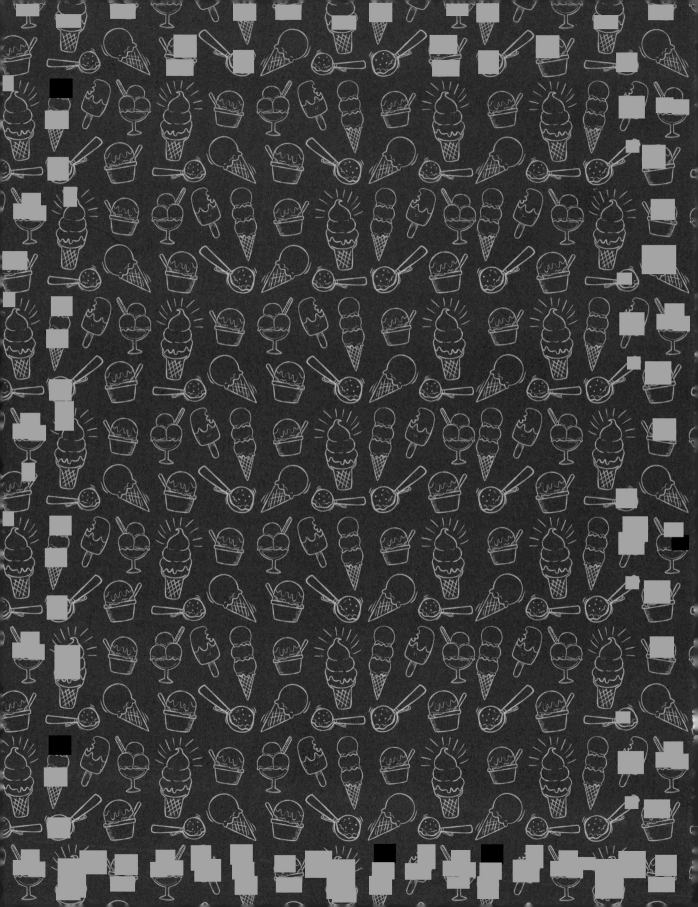